© Aladdin Books Ltd 1987

Designed and produced by
Aladdin Books Ltd
70 Old Compton Street
London W1

First published in the
United States in 1987 by
Franklin Watts
387 Park Avenue South
New York NY 10016

ISBN 0 531 10436 2

Library of Congress Catalog
Card Number: 87-50599

Printed in Belgium

Design	David West
Editor	Steve Parker
Researcher	Cecilia Weston-Baker
Illustrator	Peter Harper

The publishers wish to thank those
involved in producing this book,
especially Dr John Fry, doctor
of medicine and medical author.

Contents

UNDERSTANDING DRUGS

HEROIN

Martin Godfrey

FRANKLIN WATTS
New York · London · Toronto · Sydney

INTRODUCTION

Heroin is many things to different people. To the druggist it's an opiate chemical, a white powder made from opium poppies. To the physician it's a drug that stops pain in patients with serious illness. To thousands of other people it also stops a kind of pain – the worries and problems of everyday life. Heroin is something they take because, for a short while, it seems to bring pleasure and calmness.

But the peace and relaxation of heroin are false. Real life is always there afterwards. Heroin is an especially dangerous drug because the more of it that people take, the more they need. Before they realize it they need heroin every day, to stay alive. They are addicts. It ruins their bodies and their minds, their friendships and their families. Heroin becomes a way of life.

Nowadays heroin is more and more common in almost every country. It has also become cheaper. This means more people can afford to take it. Many people are offered a "hit of H" at some time. Maybe it's tempting to try it once, just to see what happens.

This book tells you what can happen – what heroin does to someone's body and mind. It looks at who takes heroin, and why. It also shows how heroin can creep into someone's life as an occasional "thrill," and turn into an

Publicity for the "Just Say No" campaign.

addiction that controls and finally destroys them.

This book also gives facts and advice on how heroin addicts can get help. It examines ways of getting off the drug. But the best way of stopping is – never to start.

Other names for heroin

WHY DO PEOPLE TAKE HEROIN?

***We did it just because heroin's supposed to be the ultimate kick . . .**

Heroin is taken by millions of people all over the world. Some of these are already what you might call "junkies" – in bad health, dirty clothes, no money, no jobs, nowhere to live. Others seem like ordinary people who you'd think would never touch the stuff.

Who are the first-time users?

There's no such thing as a typical first-time heroin user. However the facts show that most people who try it for the first time are between about 16 and 24 years old, and most people who use heroin have already tried some other drug.

People who take heroin may be able to give you a reason why they take it – or they may not. Some just try it because it's there. Others take it because they think it's the "in" thing to do, or because their friends take it, or because they are curious, or because they want to do something risky, or because ... there are plenty of excuses. The problem is that many people who try heroin don't know what they could be getting into. Heroin is a powerful drug, and it has led thousands of people to their deaths.

Some countries have the death penalty for being involved with heroin.

mitigating factors to spare him—Judge

HEROIN BRITON WILL HANG

LONDONER Derrick Gregory was sentenced today to hang for heroin smuggling.

HANGED

Women sob as drug Brit goes to the gall...

Cost and availability

Anyone who really wants heroin has a good chance of getting some, although they risk getting into trouble with the law. Carrying heroin, stashing it in your house, selling or buying it, and using it are all illegal acts. Punishments are severe. In some countries people who smuggle or sell heroin are put to death.

Yet heroin still gets around. The people who try it don't all come from the city, or from rich families, or poor ones, or broken homes. They are not all earning a lot, or a little, or out of work. They aren't all of a certain age and they don't all have skin of a certain color. They are not all stupid, or clever, or nervous, or successful, or failures. Heroin users may be some or all of these things.

In some areas, heroin is one of the cheaper drugs and it is easy to get hold of. On the street, it is usually mixed or "cut" with substances that bulk it up. A small bag containing around one-sixth to one-eighth of a gram of heroin (and a lot of "bulk" such as talcum powder or sugar) can cost around $10 to $20. This is enough to get a couple of people "high" for several hours.

Heroin is often sold by people who are already addicted to it. They tell you that heroin can solve your problems, and that it isn't really dangerous. They are lying.

❝ Taking H is like digging a hole for yourself. You might start digging simply because you've got a shovel. The more you dig, the deeper you get. ❞

Not knowing what it is

Some early users don't even know they are taking heroin. Many other different drugs are available, with various nicknames, and they are often surrounded by secrecy. The names and the look of heroin vary from place to place. Someone might think that it is too embarrassing to ask what "skag" or "smack" means. An interested person might think the "best" thing to do is simply to copy the others, taking the drug first and asking questions afterwards.

Being one of the crowd

Most people like to have fun. For some, this means being with friends who think in the same way, who like the same sorts of music and clothes, who like going out together. If one person in the group starts to use heroin, then before long the others in the group may be tempted to try it.

You might think: "I wouldn't touch that stuff. I've seen the ads and posters and I've seen what heroin can do to people." It is easy to say this and believe it now. But when you're in a group, and a friend tells you what a great sensation the experience was – how will you feel then?

 Everyone was talking about it and I just wanted to try it. 99

Heroin – the big one

For some people, heroin is the "big one." It has a reputation of being addictive and very dangerous. It's a challenge, and some people can't resist a challenge, even if it means running the risk of damaging yourself, of harming your health. Even more – heroin is illegal, an outlaw drug. Taking it means running the risk of being caught, which gives some people a thrill in itself.

Yet this sort of thinking is self-defeating. There are far more sensible challenges, like trying to break records on the running track or in a sport.

> ❝❝ *I suppose a lot of us were punks or ex-punks. We did it just because heroin's supposed to be the ultimate kick. It's becoming the in thing to do.* ❞❞

Life's so boring . . .

Another reason for taking heroin is to "escape." Some people think that life is boring and a drag. They may not have real friends, or much money. Or they might not have a girlfriend or boyfriend or a job. They think that heroin can be a way of forgetting their troubles. But this is nonsense. Heroin may make you feel different, for a short time, but in no way is it a solution. It's a chemical that affects the brain. It is not a way of handling the tougher parts of life. When the heroin wears off a person's troubles are still there. Drugs don't solve problems.

> ❝❝ *It's like being in your own dream world. There are no hassles, no pressures, no worrying, no tensions left around you.* ❞❞

Courage and confidence

Heroin can make some people feel that they are more self-confident. It can make them think they have the courage to go out and meet people, to talk and make friends. This is a false feeling, primarily because heroin is a depressant. The confidence is not real: it comes from a chemical and not from inside the person.

Other drugs are misused in this way, especially alcohol. People might have a few alcoholic drinks at a party, to put themselves in a lively mood and overcome their shyness. But in both cases, the confidence wears off as the drug does, and later they may regret what they did. It's no real answer.

❛❛ I always had a lack of confidence. Everything I did, I was critical of. I hated going to work because all day I would be thinking, "that's bound to be a bad decision." Then I took smack, and it seemed to help. ❜❜

Aren't people worried about taking it?

All around us are pictures of the suffering and death that heroin causes. Aren't people scared that when they take it for the first time they might get hooked?

You might think: "I'll take it only once, or twice. Addiction can't happen to me, I can control it." In fact it is easy to kid yourself. There is no way anyone can know what will happen. The heroin addicts who are at death's door thought the same as you. They weren't aiming to become addicted, yet they got hooked.

You might think: "I could never inject myself, stick a needle into my body. I'll always have to stick to smoking heroin, then I can't become addicted." This is not true. People can become addicted by smoking heroin. They can also become so dependent on the drug that they become able to inject themselves.

It all adds up

Often, heroin users say there was no one reason why they started taking the drug. There was a mixture of things, like strain at home, problems at school or work, pressure to try it from friends, boredom, no job, and so on. Heroin seemed so inviting, and under stress they could ignore all the risks and dangers. They decided to take the plunge.

Regular users

Once people have tried heroin, they can either leave it alone or use it again. Some first-timers are frightened off by the sickness (vomiting) heroin can cause. Others have satisfied their curiosity after one or two sessions. They realize that the feelings which heroin causes are not that fantastic and anyway it creates a totally false world, full of dangers. They leave it alone.

Some users take heroin when and if they can get hold of it. Maybe they have a regular date once a month, with certain friends. Perhaps they take it on vacation. They think of it as some kind of "treat," but no more.

Others go on a binge, taking heroin heavily for a few

days and then leaving it alone for months. Some drinkers use alcohol in the same way. This type of user tends to do it mainly for the buzz and doesn't see the risks involved. It is important to know that heroin can still be very dangerous when used like this.

Any of these people may go on to become regular users, once every two or three days, then once a day. They may start by sniffing or smoking the drug, but the effects soon begin to weaken. To get back the strong high, they may start to inject. This way they need a much smaller amount of heroin, which is cheaper. Often, to begin with, a friend injects for them. Some "friend." These regular users are one short, easy step from true addiction.

No one can tell, when taking heroin for the first time, how it will end. Will the first time be the only time? Will a person become an occasional user, or an addict stumbling through life toward death? The numbers of heroin addicts, and those who die from heroin addiction, speak clearly enough. That's why it is so important to say no.

WHAT DOES HEROIN DO?

"*I expected to flinch from the pain of the needle. Instead pleasure flooded through me.***"**

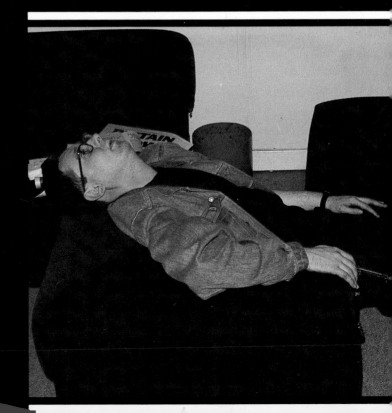

Like any drug, heroin changes the chemistry of the body. In particular, it affects the brain – where the mind is. The feelings that heroin causes are a result of this chemical action on the brain.

How is it taken?
Heroin usually comes as a powder, white or pink or brown or gray. It may be in tablets, or dissolved in water. To get the biggest effect it has to go quickly into the blood, where it then goes in a large "rush" to the brain. Heroin can be taken in four main ways with smoking and injecting having the strongest effects.

Swallowing It's simply eaten. Not much effect – most of the drug is destroyed in the stomach before it can get into the blood.

Snorting or sniffing The powder is sniffed up the nose, like cocaine or snuff. It goes through the nose lining into the blood and is carried to the brain.

Smoking (chasing the dragon) Heroin powder on metal foil is heated from underneath and the smoke is breathed in through a straw. It goes into the lungs, and quickly through their thin lining into the blood and to the brain.

Injecting, fixing or shooting up Powder is dissolved in water and injected using a needle and syringe. It's put just under the skin ("skin popping"), or into a muscle or straight into a vein ("mainlining").

Occasional users tend to smoke. Many heavy users end up mainlining, partly because this seems to be the most efficient way of getting the drug to the brain. So they get the strongest effect for the least amount of drug – which means the least amount of money.

Sickness

For some people, especially first-timers, there's a terrible feeling of sickness (nausea) after taking heroin. Some takers even throw up. It may discourage them from trying it again.

❝ *The first time I tried it, it was no good, it was so strong, the feelings rushed through me. I felt ill, sick. It really put me off. Someone said the second time was better.* ❞

Freedom from pain and worry

Heroin can take away the really severe pain of illnesses such as cancer. Many people believe that in the same way it can take away worry. While the drug is having its effect, any problems seem to become tiny or disappear altogether. Although the drug blocks them out for a short while, the problems or worries are still there.

❝ *Heroin seemed like the answer. I thought I'd take it for a bit, to get through those few weeks. Then I seemed to find more things to escape from, like pressure at work . . .* ❞

A false feeling of pleasure

Within seconds of taking heroin, there's a feeling of pleasure, warmth, joy – people feel it in different ways. It's called a "hit," "buzz," "rush" and many other names. It only lasts a short time, perhaps a few minutes, but this is long enough for some people to want to try the drug again.

I expected to flinch from the pain of the needle. Instead, pleasure flooded through me.

Crashing out

Following the rush of heroin comes a sense of calmness and relaxation. Users who've taken only a small amount can walk around and talk, seeming free and easy. With a larger dose they may lie around half-awake, in a stupor. Higher still and they crash out and may lapse into unconsciousness. With even more – an overdose – heroin can "relax" someone to death.

Nodding out was the best part. If I got the dose right it would be like dreaming . . . pictures popped into my head, then faded away . . . I'd come up for a while, then go off again.

How much is enough?

Depending on how heroin is taken, and the amount, its effects last up to several hours. But part of the problem is

Crashing out is dangerous – users may choke on their own vomit.

that people react differently to the same dose. If they have been taking a lot of heroin, and then they stop for a while, their bodies become less used to the drug. So if they come to take their old dose again, it could be an overdose.

Also, there is no way most takers can know how much real heroin is in their dose. The powder might be nine-tenths talc or flour. These "bulking" materials may have a bad effect on the user, and they have been known to kill.

All this makes it very hard to predict the effects of a given amount of "score." The only safe dose is no dose.

ILLNESSES THAT HEROIN BRINGS

" *In some big cities, most of the regular drug-takers now have AIDS.* **"**

The effects of heroin itself are only one small part of taking the drug. Its use can lead to various problems, in the body and mind, as well as deadly diseases and addiction.

The serious problems start when people take the drug regularly. Heroin tends to make you lose your appetite, so you don't eat properly. If you are using a lot, you find yourself spending every last penny (and more) in order to buy it -- so you can't afford much food anyway.

Before long, regular users start to lose weight. Their general health begins to fail, and with it their natural defenses against disease. They can become so careless that they don't really bother about looking after themselves. Their hair and clothes get dirty. They don't wash, they begin to smell, and they may catch lice and similar bugs.

A combination of poor hygiene and a bad diet is a recipe for disaster.

Dirt and squalor make serious infections more likely.

The dangers of injecting

Injecting is a major danger in itself. When doctors use a needle and syringe, they are new ones taken from a sterile pack. They are free from germs. Drug users often cannot get sterile needles. The ones they use become infected with germs. Sores, ulcers and abscesses tend to develop at the injection sites.

Once a vein has been injected several times, it swells up and gets hard or it gets soft and collapses. The user can't make it "stand up" to get the needle in properly, so further injections become very difficult. Gradually the veins in the arms are used up and then in the legs and groin.

Some heroin users share needles with others, or use "dirty" needles that they keep or find lying around. Although these needles may look clean, they will almost certainly carry germs to the skin and into the body. Heroin itself is serious enough, but sharing needles or using dirty ones is courting death, especially with the statistics surrounding the AIDS crisis.

Blood poisoning

If the body's defenses are low, or if a large number of germs are injected, then germs can spread into the blood stream to produce blood poisoning (septicemia). This is a very serious infection that can spread to affect the heart, the lungs and many other parts of the body. Untreated, it can be a killer.

The first sign of septicemia is usually a sudden fever. The sufferer gets hot and then cold and starts shivering violently. Small bruises may develop all over the body and the heart's pumping begins to fail. Urgent treatment with antibiotic medicines by a doctor is needed. But once infected, organs such as the heart become permanently damaged and never work properly again. This can lead to health problems in later life.

Heroin use brings with it many problems and illnesses.

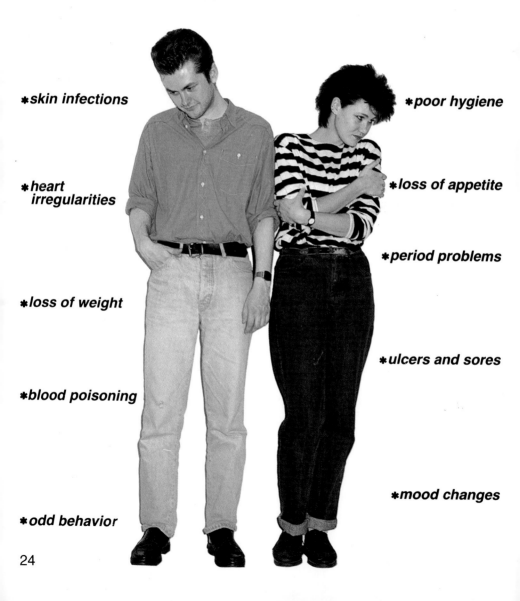

＊skin infections

＊poor hygiene

＊heart irregularities

＊loss of appetite

＊period problems

＊loss of weight

＊ulcers and sores

＊blood poisoning

＊mood changes

＊odd behavior

Hepatitis B

Another serious infection spread by shared or dirty needles is hepatitis B. The germs get into the blood and can produce yellowing of the skin and eyes (jaundice), cancer of the liver, and even death.

Unfortunately it may be impossible to tell if a person is infected with hepatitis B. Some people are "carriers" of this disease, which means they are infected by the germs and can pass them on, but they have no symptoms. There is no sure way of avoiding hepatitis B if shared or dirty needles are used.

AIDS

AIDS (Acquired-Immune Deficiency Syndrome) is very much in the news. Heroin abuse is one of the ways of catching it. The AIDS virus (the germ that causes AIDS) is transferred by using a needle which has been infected by someone who already has it.

But, as with hepatitis B, there is often no outward sign that someone is carrying the AIDS virus. So with both these diseases it is impossible to avoid infection if needles are shared. In some big cities, most of the regular drug takers now have the AIDS virus. The majority will probably go on to develop AIDS itself. (Women are just as likely to get AIDS in this way as men are.) So far, no one has recovered from AIDS. In the United States about 3,000 drug addicts have AIDS, 17% of the total number of people with the illness. The sexual partners of these drug addicts are all at high risk of contacting the AIDS virus.

Needles

If people could be persuaded not to share needles or equipment, or not to use dirty needles, some of the problems associated with injecting could be avoided. Unfortunately, in many countries needles are expensive and are only available from doctors. Users may find that needles are more difficult to get hold of than heroin itself.

In order to lessen the number of people getting these infections, particularly AIDS, some governments have now decided to let registered addicts have free needles and syringes. They hope that fewer drug users will get AIDS and that its spread will slow down. This would mean that its spread to other people, mainly by sexual contact, would also be slowed down.

Mind problems

Heavy heroin use is not an illness of the mind as such. However it can bring about a lot of unpleasant mood changes. Since heroin is a depressant, users and addicts may start to behave oddly. They can be aggressive or have sudden changes of mood, from being very happy, to terribly sad, to extremely angry. Sometimes heavy users and addicts get so depressed that they consider suicide.

People around the user can't understand these changes, which seem to happen for no reason. It becomes difficult to remain friends or to talk sensibly.

Overdose and suicide

Overdose is always a danger, even for the experienced

user. It is almost impossible to tell how much of the powder in the little bag is actually heroin. There may be all sorts of poisons and other drugs mixed in with it. And the body's tolerance level to heroin changes with time. Someone who took a lot, and who then stopped, will react far more strongly when he or she takes the "usual" dose again.

Also heroin affects the body differently when taken along with other drugs, such as alcohol. Heroin and alcohol together are a lethal combination and the cause of many deaths.

So there is no way of saying how much heroin is an overdose. Of the people who die from an overdose ("OD"), many are killed by suffocation – heroin stops them breathing.

Likewise, no one knows how many people use heroin to commit suicide. It is relatively easy to inject far too much of the drug. When the person is dead, and there are no good clues, it is difficult to know whether it was suicide or an accident.

Special problems in women
Many girls who take heroin find their periods stop or become irregular. The lifestyle associated with heroin abuse can lead to infection of the womb or fallopian tubes, and this may cause infertility.

A heroin-addicted mother can also cause problems for her unborn baby. Again, her lifestyle may mean she doesn't eat properly, which can badly affect the developing baby. If she takes heroin regularly throughout her pregnancy then

Clara Hale's New York City clinic has treated many addicted babies.

the baby will also become dependent on the drug, so that it is a heroin addict at birth. This is not a good start in life. However, with the proper medical care, the baby can be weaned off the drug.

The drug culture

Finally, heroin abusers are more likely than other people to have used other drugs, such as alcohol, nicotine (in tobacco), cocaine or marijuana. They tend to mix in groups where any drug use, illegal or legal, is considered normal. They may develop problems with other drugs as well as with heroin.

THE COST OF ADDICTION

" *Toward the end, my son threatened to kill me if I didn't give him money.* **"**

Heroin addiction is not a pretty picture. Addicts are "hooked," they have "the habit." They depend on the drug, they need it regularly – perhaps several times a day, and they have to find the money to pay for it. They try to cope, but are often forced to live the way heroin wants them to.

Some addicts get sucked into pushing and dealing. They risk deadly illnesses, overdose, prison. They don't know what is in their dose, whether it has been "spiked" with garbage or even a poison. They may lose the support of friends and family. Living in dirty conditions, they may resort to stealing or prostitution. They may lose all hope and give up. Some addicts choose being dead to being hooked.

A few addicts – but not many – manage to keep out of all this. They can do it because heroin itself, as a drug, may not actually kill. It is possible for the body to be addicted to heroin without death as a result. What usually kills is the way many people are forced to live when dependent on heroin.

How do people get hooked?

Heroin is one of the most addictive drugs known. This means it's really easy to get hooked on. Many occasional users laugh when you tell them about the risks of addiction. "It won't happen to us," they say, "we're on top of it." Yet one week they're taking heroin, thinking they've got it under control, and in a few weeks they realize they are addicted. They think they need the drug. It has a good chance of ruining their health, of bringing illnesses like hepatitis or blood poisoning, and – in the end – of killing them.

❝ *Helen was the first person to offer me heroin. She wasn't trying to get me hooked or anything. I suppose she thought she was doing me a favor, letting me in on a secret thing, which ordinary people didn't have.* **❞**

How long does it take to get hooked?

Less time than you think. People have become dependent on heroin after only a couple of weeks. For some it takes longer. But at the start, there's no way of knowing how long it will take. A lot depends on how much heroin is used, and how often, how pure it is, and how the person's body reacts to it.

The great danger is that, by the time people realize they are becoming addicts, they may not be able to stop.

How many addicts?

There are perhaps 500,000 heroin addicts in the United States. There are about 70,000 in Great Britain and similar numbers in many other countries. As heroin becomes cheaper and easier to find, the numbers are going up fast in many places. In a recent year the number of known heroin addicts in Britain increased by one half.

The body

Each time a person takes heroin, it has less effect. To get the same effect as before, more of the drug is needed each time. And more. It doesn't matter how it's taken: smoking or

The campaign against drugs: heroin screws you up.

injecting can still cause addiction.

Gradually the body becomes used to heroin. So much that, after a while, heroin has hardly any effects at all. The sense of pleasure and the forgetting of problems no longer happen. Now things are different. The body has become so used to heroin that it needs the drug just to work normally. It depends on heroin. The person has become physically addicted to the drug. Take it away, and the body reacts with all the pain and anguish of withdrawal.

The mind

Not only the body comes to depend on heroin. The mind may become dependent on it too – often before the body does. The user begins to think that he or she can't get through the day without heroin and the buzz it gives.

People might start out by using heroin occasionally, as

a special treat. Then they might begin to make up reasons why they need it. Maybe it's going to be a particularly bad day, they have to meet some one , or see the boss at work, or visit parents, or ask for money.

Some users see the danger coming and make up "rules" for themselves, like taking the drug only for three days and then having two days off. But more and more they find reasons to break the rules. To them, life without heroin seems so dull and boring.

*** I got to thinking about the disco . . . it would be much better if I took some, I'd enjoy it much more, be confident, more impressive. I knew how dangerous this sort of thinking was, but I couldn't stop. In the end I did go out and score, and I did have a good time. But I knew, inside, it was the worst mistake.* **

The financial cost

One shot of heroin may not cost much. But for the addict, heroin is never cheap. The amount needed depends on how long the addiction has lasted and how the body itself is putting up with the drug. Some addicts keep going on a fifth of a gram a day. For those who have to take a lot, the cost may be up to two days' worth of salary – each day. Few people can afford to pay for their habit legally, unless they have a family fortune or they have a well-paid job and they can take time off work whenever they want.

For many addicts, the only way to pay for their habit is

Prostitution is one way that some women finance their drug buying.

by crime. They steal or sell stolen goods. They may become prostitutes, or pimps. When heroin itself is so important, other people are not. Addicts steal from family, friends, other users – whoever they can.

Some addicts turn to dealing in heroin itself, since they need it anyway and they develop the connections. They buy a batch of the drug, use some of it, and try to sell the rest at a profit in order to buy the next batch.

> ❢❢ **The family silver was in the dining room, locked in a cupboard. We hardly ever used it. I took a few pieces, went to the next town and traded them. No one noticed at first.** ❣❣

The costs to health

As heroin takes over, everything else suffers. Some addicts don't care about eating properly, or keeping clean, or how they look. They become thin and pale, with spots and sores on their skin and dirty hair. If they inject, their arms and legs become bruised, swollen and infected. They risk many serious, even deadly, diseases. They often haven't got enough money to buy good food or clothes. As they mix more with other addicts, looking good and feeling fit don't seem to matter anymore.

❝❝ *When we finally tracked him down, he looked so ill. We wanted him to come home, but he said no, it was only a bad cold, he would get better. Afterwards his father and I talked about it. We didn't believe him.* **❞❞**

The cost to others
It's well known that a junkie cannot be a reliable friend. Heroin is usually far too important to let friendship or family ties interfere with getting it. Some addicts lie, steal, rip each other off. They threaten their parents, old friends, passers-by, even children. Some kill for their addiction.

❝❝ *Toward the end, my son threatened to kill me if I didn't give him money. I was in such a state, I think he really meant it. I didn't know what to do. I was desperate to help, but I didn't want him to get arrested and put in jail . . . what a choice.* **❞❞**

Managing the habit
A few people can be heroin addicts and somehow live a kind

of normal life. This is what many users hope when they realize they are becoming dependent and they think they can't stop themselves. But it is very difficult. They need money, a lot of friendship and support, and to be kept away from the temptation to use the drug. Unfortunately heroin works against all these things.

Withdrawal

When an addict suddenly stops taking heroin, the body and mind react badly. A few addicts say that coming off heroin, or "coming clean," is like getting a bad cold. But for most it is worse. It's the fear of withdrawal, or "cold turkey," that keeps some of them on the drug.

Deprived of heroin, and without proper care, the typical addict gets twitchy, edgy, and uneasy a few hours after the last dose. The addict wants H and may get very frightened. He or she may try to delay things by using another drug, like drinking cough medicine or alcohol, or taking speed (amphetamines). But the delaying tactics won't work for long. The addict begins to tremble, sweat, yawn and sneeze. The person's skin feels ice-cold and small spots appear, like goose pimples (this is where the name comes from – "cold turkey"). The eyes and nose run and the body aches all over and feels weak and cold. There are pains in the stomach, arms and legs. The person feels feels sick and may throw up. For some addicts this lasts less than a day, for others it may mean several days. Gradually the effects fade away. But the edginess and difficulty in sleeping can last for several weeks.

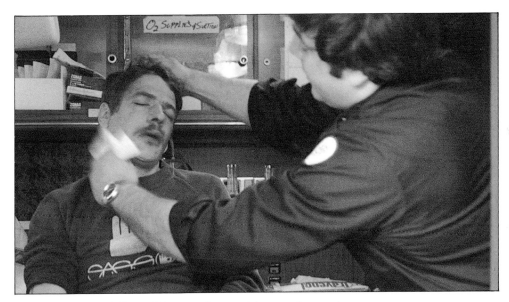

Expert care and first aid ease the problems of overdose.

Stories about withdrawal stop some addicts from trying to give up heroin. They imagine the nightmare of being arrested for possession and then going through withdrawal locked up, alone, in a prison cell. Nowadays, with proper help, this needn't be so. Addicts do manage to get off heroin, and withdrawal isn't necessarily a nightmare.

What happens to addicts?

It is difficult to know what eventually happens to heroin addicts. Many live in a twilight world, not talking to their family and without friends. It's hard to get reliable facts.

Some studies have been carried out, mainly by drug treatment centers in big cities like New York, London and Paris. They show that on average, of 10 addicts coming to a treatment center, after 10 years:

Two of the 10 would be dead. Addicts can die in any one of many ways, from an overdose to a serious disease such as hepatitis or AIDS or to a street fight over the drug.

Four of the 10 would still be addicted. They may have tried to come off heroin, and even succeeded for a time. For these four people the future looks grim.

The other four of the 10 would be off heroin. Their health would probably be improving and their outlook would be good.

MANUFACTURE, TRADE AND CRIME

"Heroin used by a human being produces an unmoral savage . . . who . . . becomes cold-blooded and capable of committing any crime."

Heroin is made from a plant, the opium poppy. Under the petals is a large pod, like a hen's egg. Slit the unripe pod and a milky juice seeps out. This gradually sets into a brownish putty or resin, which is called opium. Opium contains several drugs, including morphine. Chemists purify the morphine and then combine it with other chemicals to make heroin.

Halfway to heroin: a Chinese opium den, in 1907.

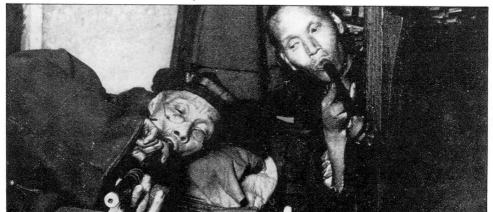

The search for better medicines

Opium has been smoked, eaten, or drunk as a tea for thousands of years, especially in the Middle and Far East. It gave relief from pain, it was used to treat disease, and it worked as a magical potion to alter the mind. Only a few hundred years ago opium was in common use across the world. In those times people had few of the medicines we have today, and if you were really ill, anything was worth a try.

But opium was a poor medicine. It made some people

feel sick, while others became addicted. This was why chemists wanted to purify the different drugs in it.

Morphine was ten times stronger than opium. It blocked pain better, and did not make users feel so sick. It quickly became a favorite with doctors. But it too had side effects and turned people into addicts. So the search went on for a better version. In 1874, in London, heroin was first made.

The rise and fall of heroin

In the 1880s heroin started to be more widely used. It was stronger than morphine and became an important drug in medicine. During World War I it helped relieve terrible pain for thousands of men injured in the fighting.

Very quickly, though, people saw how harmful and addictive heroin could be. By the 1920s the United States had perhaps 250,000 heroin addicts. Many became addicted to the drug while fighting in World War I. Crime was also involved as rival gangs fought to control the heroin trade and keep the profits. Doctors swiftly changed their minds. Heroin was no longer a miracle cure. As a result, heroin was banned in the United States in 1924.

Heroin compared to other drugs

Heroin is an illegal drug in every country. If you are caught carrying it, you are in big trouble. In some countries people who smuggle it, or simply possess it, are put to death. In 1987 two Australians were hanged in Malaysia for smuggling the drug.

Yet is heroin so different from other drugs, like alcohol? The short answer is: yes, heroin is different.

There are plenty of legal drugs, ones that can be bought over the counter, that affect the mind. Alcohol, for instance, can make you feel happy and relaxed, and it can deaden pain. But it can also kill. Tobacco, which contains the drug nicotine, is also legal. If you are old enough you can buy a pack of cigarettes. Yet as you smoke each cigarette you are shortening your life by an average of five minutes, by increasing the risks of a heart attack, or lung cancer or bronchitis.

So what's the difference? Alcohol appears more acceptable, partly because it was the first on the scene. People have been making alcoholic drinks for thousands of years, and they became too popular to ban. Even during the Prohibition years of the 1920s, drinking was not wiped out – simply driven underground.

Tobacco is less easy to explain. Its short-term effects are very mild, and only recently have doctors linked it with serious diseases. In the meantime it has become a social habit and also big business. Yet the tide is turning against tobacco in many countries. Trains, theaters and other public places are becoming no-smoking areas. Slowly people are recognizing how dangerous it is.

Enforcing the law

When heroin was made illegal, the hope was that fewer people would try it. Severe punishments were society's way of warning against the dangers of heroin abuse.

However not everyone agreed with this approach. The laws were often used against individual heroin takers rather than the large-scale dealers who were the real menace. Also the laws meant that heroin abuse became a problem to be sorted out by the police, rather than by doctors or social workers.

The same arguments still go on. "Heroin used by a human being produces an unmoral savage . . . who . . . becomes cold-blooded and capable of committing any crime." This was an American doctor – speaking not today, as you might think, but in 1920.

Many heroin addicts end up in trouble with the law, not only for possessing or trading or smuggling the drug. Some get mixed up in stealing, mugging and prostitution. Crime is the only way to finance their addiction, and many are forced to steal . . . sometimes from family and friends.

❝ *Abe seemed to disappear, we didn't see him for a couple of weeks. Then the police came and told us he'd been living rough in the wood, in an old shed up at the back.* ❞

Where is heroin made?

Opium poppies are grown where the weather and soil are warm and fairly dry, mainly in Southeast Asia and in the border area between northern Pakistan and Afghanistan. These places are called the "Golden Triangle" and the "Golden Crescent."

Local farmers grow the poppies, slit the ripe pods,

scrape up the opium resin which oozes out, and sell it. Most poppy-growing is illegal but the law finds it difficult to keep a check on every farm in these hilly, remote places.

Turning opium into morphine, and then into heroin, is done in heroin "factories" or "laboratories" near where the poppies grow. They are usually dirty, rough-and-ready places. Soldiers and police regularly find factories and destroy them, but new ones soon spring up. Recently the Pakistan authorities closed down 41 heroin factories in one year, but there was little effect on the amounts of heroin being made.

The trade in heroin

Heroin is a business. It is grown, harvested, bought and sold – all against the law. People make big money out of it, which is why the trade is so difficult to stamp out.

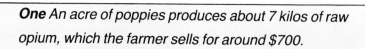

One An acre of poppies produces about 7 kilos of raw opium, which the farmer sells for around $700.

Two In a local "factory" the raw opium is made into heroin. It is now worth about $70,000.

Three The heroin powder is smuggled into the country by a "courier." In the dealer network its value is approximately $450,000.

Four The heroin is "cut" and divided up into little bags to sell on the street. It will bring in $1,500,000. Not many businesses make so much profit at each stage.

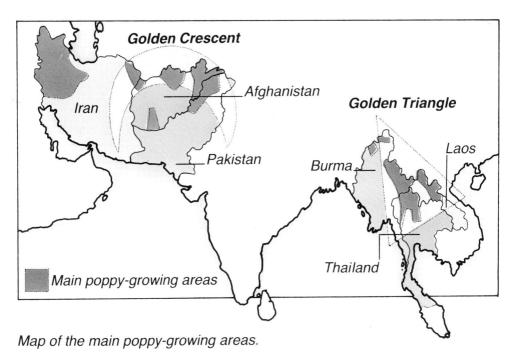

Map of the main poppy-growing areas.

The growers

For the farmers and their families, opium poppies are their livelihood. A farmer in northwest Pakistan might make $700 a year for his acre of opium poppies. A thin crop of wheat from the same soil might fetch $20. When officials from Europe or the United States go to poppy-growing areas to try and change things, they are not very welcome.

The profits from heroin are often spent not on food or clothes but on guns and other weapons. In the war between the USSR and the Afghanistan rebel fighters, the rebels have used "poppy profits" to buy their armaments. These are often supplied by the countries where the heroin was smuggled to. It's a sort of extremely brutal "fair swop" – death for death.

Supply and smuggling

The United States is supplied mainly from the Golden Triangle area. Much of the traffic began when American soldiers took the drug during the Vietnam war, and the trade followed them home. The Golden Crescent supplies most of Europe. Heroin is so profitable that people in other countries are increasing production: Lebanon and Syria, Colombia in South America, Mexico and in the Caribbean.

Light, fluffy heroin powder can be hidden away almost anywhere. It is smuggled in an ever-changing list of ways – hidden in furniture or suitcases, in the seats of cars, inside cameras, sewn into clothes, in babies' buggies, even in plastic bags inside living animals.

The people who smuggle heroin are called couriers, or "mules." Some of them swallow small bags of heroin, travel, and then watch the lavatory until the bags appear. Thieves have slit them open to steal their heroin. Sometimes a bag bursts inside the courier, who dies from a massive heroin overdose.

The profits are so great that there's plenty of money to attempt to bribe airline staffs, customs people or ship employees. In exchange for money they agree to "look the other way" as a heroin shipment passes through. Customs officers and police have had some success. They may act on a tip off or use sniffer dogs to smell out drugs wrapped tightly in plastic inside a suitcase. But not all shipments come through main ports and airports. Some are landed from small boats at remote beaches at night or flown into a local airfield in a small private plane.

There are simply not enough coast guards, police and customs officers to search every person, suitcase and crate. Police chiefs admit that the amounts of heroin they seize are only a fraction of the total being smuggled.

Pushers and dealers

Once heroin is smuggled into a country, it enters the network of dealers and pushers. People cheat, lie and murder to get their hand on a shipment, which can easily be worth many millions of dollars. Then the heroin is mixed with another powder, like chalk, sugar or flour. What is supposed to be pure heroin on the streets may contain as little as

The Coast Guard seizes a drugs shipment, but others slip through.

one-tenth of actual heroin.

Pushers, like couriers, are at the "sharp" end of the business. They are the ones that run the risks. They may be addicts themselves, dealing in heroin to keep their habits going. They are mixed up in a shady world where their "customers," given half a chance, will stab them in the back.

Hidden behind their assistants and bodyguards are the "drug barons" and the big-time dealers. The barons control the manufacture and distribution of heroin, and probably other drugs as well. The big-time dealers smuggle in shipments and pass them through the network to small-time pushers on the streets. The barons and big dealers are rich and powerful, and they will stop at nothing.

Another shady deal is struck at the end of the heroin chain.

GETTING HELP

"Smack takes away the pain of life, but it also takes away the pleasure."

Taking heroin regularly, or being addicted, is not a disease. It's not something you catch, like a cold that will go away by itself or that can be "cured" by taking medicines. If you're the one who is taking heroin, then stopping depends mainly on you. Help and support are available from many places, but the most important thing is your own will to stop and your determination to keep off the drug.

Saying no is the only sure way of not becoming an addict.

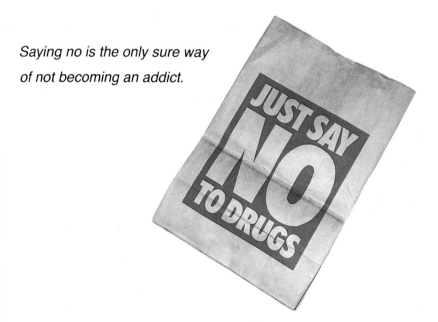

Occasional takers

Statistics show that most people who take heroin only do so once or a few times. They may be offered some by a friend, or it s being used at a party.It might feel good at the time, but once or twice is enough. These people understand the dangers of heroin, they see what a false world it creates, and they don't need that sort of problem. They soon leave it alone.

More regular users

People who take heroin more regularly, perhaps once a day for a few weeks or months, may get slight withdrawal symptoms when they stop. But they do stop. They soon come to realize that they can do without the drug. The thought of asking for help from their families, their doctors or drug counselors just doesn't enter their head. It's not a problem – they have caught it in time.

People who are thinking about taking heroin more often, and who believe they will be the users who can simply drop it, could well be fooling themselves. Heroin is such a powerful substance that it can change the way you think and act. It can rub out the will to stop taking it, and you won't even have noticed.

Heavy users and addicts

Of the people who try heroin at least once (the "ever-users"), about 2 in 10 become addicts. Like the other 8, they thought they could control it. They thought they could stop whenever they liked. But at the time they didn't really want to. Now their lives are in chaos and their health is bad. They want help.

For many heavy users and addicts, the thought of coming clean and facing life without the support of "their drug" is too much. They want to be well but secretly, inside themselves, they don't want to stop taking heroin. These people need an extra effort to admit the real problem to themselves.

Experience shows that people can stop taking heroin when they want to. About one in five American soldiers who

fought in Vietnam took heroin at some time. Yet on their return, about seven out of eight of these users gave it up. The pressure was off and they didn't need the drug any more.

Admitting it to yourself

Strangely, it may take a long time before regular users admit to themselves that they are addicted to heroin. It can take even longer before they do anything about it. Fears have probably grown up about the horrors of cold turkey (withdrawal), so that addicts may try to stay on heroin rather than risk what they think will be a nightmare experience.

Deciding to come off heroin

First, you must decide you really want to stop. Next, you should ask for help. Most people like to help others, and they'll act when asked. Heroin abuse is no longer the unmentionable it used to be – most people realize that users and addicts need help, not punishment. There are many people you can approach: members of your family, a close relative, a good friend, a family doctor, a local priest, rabbi or other church person, a teacher, or a youth leader.

Maybe you'd rather talk to someone out of the local area, someone who isn't involved and who doesn't know you. In this case try: any doctor, a drug counselor, a social worker, or any of the drug agencies or hotlines listed at the back of this book. Waiting to help are many people, and

The pressures of the Vietnam War drove many soldiers to drugs.

many organizations run by professionals, by volunteers or by medical or church people. But they don't come looking for customers. You must make the first move.

The doctor

Your local family doctor is a good person to see first. He or she will check you over to see what your health is like. You can then be treated, either by the doctor or at a unit for drug-takers.

If, on the other hand, you don't want to contact people who may know you, you can go to any one of the clinics or agencies throughout the United States. Many of them are listed in the yellow pages and offer confidential help by people who know what they are talking about.

Treatments

One of the main treatments used by doctors to get people off heroin is with another drug, called methadone. It is similar to heroin but its effects last longer, so it needs to be used only once a day. The length of treatment during this detoxification stage varies, but it can be from as little as four to six weeks or as long as a year or more.

Methadone is taken as a syrup, so there's no need to take the drug intravenously. This helps cut down on the dangers of contaminated needles. As the patient improves, the dose is reduced and eventually dropped completely. Another drug, naltrexone, is sometimes used instead of methadone.

Some heavy users and addicts, can come off the drug

at home. They see the doctor each day to get their next day's prescription. Those who are taking high doses of heroin, may go each day to a drug dependency clinic for prescription and advice. Others stay at the clinic while they gradually come off heroin.

Occasionally the drug dependency units may use various techniques. One is acupuncture, when special needles are put in various parts of the body to try and ease away discomfort (no drugs are injected).

All in all, coming off heroin may not be very pleasant. But if people use the various methods available today, the symptoms can be controlled to some extent. Many people now find it more bearable and not the nightmare it's made out to be.

Staying off heroin

Once a person is off heroin, there is still more work to be done. Many addicts try to stop several times, only to start again when they start mixing with their old friends and when their old problems come back again. In most cases, the only ways addicts will truly kick the habit are to make some real changes in their lives – to kick the old lifestyle as well, to get rid of all drug associations and temptations. Trying to give up heroin is even harder when you are still surrounded by people who are taking it. To make these changes, most addicts need some help.

Family and friends play an important part. Families Anonymous is an organization that gives advice to the relatives of addicts, helping them to support each other.

William O'Donnell, ex-addict and rehab pioneer, greets a client.

Most addicts are also encouraged to join Narcotics Anonymous, which can support them after they come off heroin or after a stay at a rehabilitation center. Advice is given by ex-addicts, who have kicked the problem and are willing to pass on their experience.

"Rehab"

Many addicts go to rehabilitation (rehab) centers. The center aims to restore people's self-discipline and with it their self-respect. The hope is that drug abusers can learn to live a normal life, without the need to use drugs as a support or crutch.

You must be drug-free to enter a rehab center. Once in, you join what's called a "therapeutic community." This is a big friendly group, like a large family. All the addicts and ex-addicts who live in the center join together as a self-help group. They talk about their feelings and their experiences. In the process they learn from each other and they help each other to cope without heroin.

The outlook

After 10 years of treatment, many drug centers report that about 2 addicts in 10 are now completely free of the drug. Some centers have better results – as high as 8 addicts in 10 have steered clear of 'H.'

There are no quick solutions to the problems of heroin addiction. A "cure" usually needs years of hard work, by addicts themselves and by other people, not only in the medical world but social workers, police, teachers, youth workers – and not least, family and friends. But heroin can be kicked, and you can get back to living a normal life.

❝ *Heroin takes away the pain, for a while, but then it becomes pain. Every morning was the same, wake up, get a shot into you, out to try and make a few bucks, then score. When I finally got off I began to come alive again, notice the weather, actually talk to people . . .* **❞**

FACTFILE

What heroin looks like

Pure heroin is white and comes as a powder, in tablets, as a liquid (linctus) or in sealed glass capsules (ampoules).

Heroin bought illegally from street dealers is usually impure and in the form of a powder, or granules, like cat litter. It can range in color from white through cream to yellow, pink, light or dark brown or gray, depending on what was used to mix it to bulk it out. There is no accurate way of knowing its purity other than by proper laboratory analysis.

"Tasting" a small dab of it, as shown in some films and on television, is not a precise way of identifying heroin and can be dangerous.

Various types of heroin powder.

Tell-tale signs of heroin abuse

If you suspect someone of secretly using heroin, there are several tell-tale signs which include:

● a hidden stash of equipment which could be used to take heroin, such as matches and tinfoil or a spoon for smoking, straws for sniffing or needles, syringes, cotton or tissues (perhaps bloodstained) for injecting

● small plastic bags or folded paper bags ("cling bags" or "wraps" or "deals") used to hold the powder. Odd behavior, not answering questions openly, being vague about friends and going out, being sleepy and unable to concentrate, always broke, lying, stealing

● small red marks (injection marks or "tracking marks") on the arms or legs, skin spots and sores, loss of interest in personal appearance, poor hygiene

Items which could indicate heroin use.

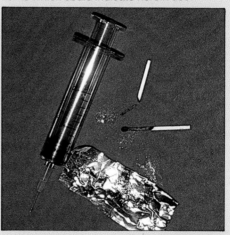

Emergency!

If someone gets into real trouble with heroin, such as becoming unconscious, the best advice is to send or telephone for an ambulance or get some other form of emergency medical care. While waiting, place the person in the recovery position shown below. This way, if he is sick, he is less likely to choke on the vomit.

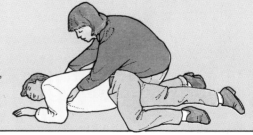

DRUG PROFILE

Common name	Heroin	*Numbers of*	Estimated number of
Chemical name	Diacetyl morphine	*users*	regular users in the
Drug type	Analgesic (pain-killer)		United States: 600,000.
Other names	H, skat, skag, gear, junk	*Example of*	Sells for about $1.40 a
	and others	*cost*	milligram. A $10 bag is
Made from	Opium resin (from the		made up of about 15
	opium poppy) refined to		milligrams.
	morphine and then	*Legal status*	Class 1 Controlled
	chemically changed to		substance
	heroin	*Examples of*	Articles 220 and 221 of
Ways of taking	Eating (not much	*penalties*	the Penal Law deal
	effect), sniffing/snorting		penalties with the
	(mild effect), smoking		unlawful trade in mind-
	fumes and injecting (big		affecting drugs. These
	effect)		articles are compatible
Main effects	Blocks pain; short-lived		with the Public Health
	feeling of pleasure (the		Law. They set criminal
	"buzz"), temporary		penalties for possession
	feelings of calm and		or sale of drugs
	freedom from worry		considered harmful or
Addictiveness	One of the most		subject to abuse. Such
	addictive drugs known,		a drug is heroin. The
	both physically and		penalty can vary from a
	mentally		misdemeanor (which
Risks	Damage to veins;		can mean up to 3
	diseases such as		months in jail or a $500
	hepatitis and AIDS		fine) to an A-1 Felony,
	spread by shared/dirty		which carries a
	needles; malnutrition,		minimum term of 15 to
	skin and hair problems;		25 years and a life term
	menstrual problems in		maximum. The
	women; mental		seriousness of the
	problems; death from		penalty depends upon
	overdose, suicide, etc.;		the individual drug and
	general dangers of		the amount held or sold.
	"druggie" lifestyle,		
	trouble with the law		
Main producer	Pakistan/Afghanistan/		
countries	Iran (Golden Crescent)		
	Burma/Laos/Thailand		
	(Golden Triangle)		
Main consumer	Becoming widespread		
countries	in most developed		
	countries especially		
	USA, Canada, Britain		
	and Europe, Australia,		
	Soviet Union		

SOURCES OF HELP

Here are addresses and telephone numbers of organizations who might be able to help people with a heroin problem.

National Hotlines
National Institute on Drug Abuse
Treatment Referral
1-(800) 622-H-E-L-P
This hotline is staffed from 9.00am to 3.00am on weekdays and from 12 noon to 3.00am on weekends. Counselors can talk with you, refer you to a drug treatment program, or answer questions about drugs, rehabilitation, health or legal problems.
New York State Division of Substance
Abuse Services
1-(800) 522-5353
This toll-free number reaches counselors who can provide referrals for treatment or legal advice, or over-the-telephone crisis intervention.
National Federation of Parents for Drug
Free Youth
1-(800) 554-K-I-D-S
This is not a crisis hotline, but a place to call for drug information. This educational organization provides both parents and kids with informational pamphlets, books and videos.

Drug Treatment and Rehabilitation Programs
There are 8,000 to 10,000 drug treatment programs across the country. These include inpatient (residential) and outpatient facilities, covering a range of services: detoxification, counseling, family intervention, after-care. Call one of the national hotlines to find a program near you. Also, your local hospital may be able to direct you to a methadone or other treatment program. Or check the Yellow Pages under Drug Abuse and Addiction.

Self-Help Organizations
National Self Help Clearinghouse
33 W. 42nd Street
New York, NY 10036
(212) 840-1259
Can provide information on self-help rehabilitation organizations in your area, or put you in touch with one of the twenty-seven state and local self-help clearinghouses around the country.
Narcotics Anonymous World Service
Office
PO Box 9999
Van Nuys, Cal. 91409
In NA group meetings, recovered addicts help recovering addicts solve their problems. You do not have to be off drugs any length of time before you participate; the only requirement is the desire to stop using drugs. Local groups are listed in the phone book.
Families Anonymous
PO Box 528
Van Nuys, Cal. 91408
A support group for families of people who abuse drugs. The national office can direct you to meetings near you.

Referrals, Information and More
Hale House for Infants
68 Edgecombe Avenue
New York, NY 10031
(212) 690-5623
This Harlem, New York, center takes care of the children of drug addicts.
Freedom from Chemical Dependency
26 Cross Street
Needham, Mass. 02194
Besides conducting drug prevention workshops in schools for faculty and students, this organization offers "evaluations" – after two meetings, a counselor can refer the client to an appropriate drug program. Also provides family intervention.

WHAT THE WORDS MEAN

addict someone who needs to keep taking a drug in order to remain "normal" and stave off withdrawal effects on the body and/or mind. "Addiction" has a slightly different meaning to "dependence," in that it usually refers to someone who has been dependent on a drug for some time, and it is more tied up with a person's lifestyle and society's view of that person. In some countries "addict" is a legal term, meaning someone who's registered on an official list as being dependent on a drug

analgesic drug that stops or reduces pain

dependence the need to keep taking a drug regularly, either for its effects on the body (to keep away withdrawal symptoms, for instance) or its effects on the mind (such as to make users think they are "getting through the day")

diacetyl morphine chemical name for heroin

drug any chemical or other substance that changes the body's workings (including the way the person's mind works, the person's behavior, etc.)

drug abuse drug use with harmful effects on the abuser and possibly on others

drug misuse using drugs in a way which people in general would see as not sensible, or not acceptable, and possibly harmful

methadone a powerful analgesic drug similar to morphine. It is sometimes used as a replacement for heroin during treatment of people dependent on heroin. It prevents the onset of withdrawal symptoms but does not give the "rush" of heroin

morphine a powerful analgesic drug extracted from opium resin, used in medicine to relieve severe pain. It tends to cause nausea (feeling sick) so it is not often abused

opium raw opium is a jelly- or putty-like brownish substance collected from the seed heads of opium poppy flowers. When processed it may be a brown powder or a thick dark syrup. It contains the analgesic drugs morphine and codeine, as well as many other substances

overdose too much of a drug for a particular person at a particular time, which causes serious effects such as breathing troubles, heart problems and possibly death. Regular users can build up tolerance; after a break, when they lose the tolerance, if they take the "old" dose again it could be an overdose

tolerance when the body becomes used to a drug, so that the same dose begins to have less effect, and increasing doses must be taken for the same effect

withdrawal the effects on the body and mind when a person suddenly stops taking a drug after being dependent on it. The effects are usually unpleasant, such as hallucinations, sickness, aches and pains, and so on

INDEX

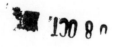